G is for Golden Boy

A Manitoba Alphabet

Written by Larry Verstraete and Illustrated by Brian Lund

Sleeping Bear Press™
310 North Main Street, Suite 300
Chelsea, MI 48118
www.sleepingbearpress.com

© 2009 Sleeping Bear Press is an imprint of Gale, a part of Cengage Learning.

Printed and bound in China.

First Edition

10 9 8 7 6 5 4 3 2 1

Library of Congress Cataloging-in-Publication Data

Verstraete, Larry.
G is for Golden Boy : a Manitoba alphabet / written by Larry Verstraete;
illustrated by Brian Lund.
p. cm.
Summary: "From A to Z the history, culture, landscapes, famous people and
provincial symbols are introduced. Each letter topic is explained through a
simple poem. Expository text gives further details about each topic. Manitoba
topics include, beluga whales, Ella Cora Hind, heritage festivals, Kitchie Manitou,
and Turtle Mountain"—Provided by publisher.
ISBN 978-1-58536-364-3
1. Manitoba—Juvenile literature. I. Lund, Brian. II. Title.

F1062.4.V47 2009
971.27—dc22
2008040929

For my wife, Jo, my soul-mate
and companion on life's journey.

For my parents, George and Paula,
who settled in Manitoba and started it all.

LARRY

To my wife Edmée,
who believed in and encouraged me.

To my grandchildren, Gavin, Brinley,
Myles, and Lindsey, my inspiration.

BRIAN

Our watery past is everywhere
in ridges, dunes, and fossil traces.
A stands for the Ancient Shores
that lie beneath our places.

A a

For most of its history, what is now Manitoba has been under water and ice. Four hundred and fifty million years ago, a vast, warm sea covered much of the area. The sea eventually drained. Then twenty thousand years ago, during the most recent Ice Age, the land was buried under a massive ice sheet, three kilometres deep in places. As the ice melted and retreated, it pulverized bedrock, plopped boulders in odd places, carved giant potholes in the soil, and created a 1,100 kilometre by 320 kilometre lake known as Lake Agassiz.

Lake Agassiz eventually drained and disappeared, but signs of Manitoba's watery origins are everywhere. Ridges and sand dunes mark places where shorelines and deltas once existed, and fossils of extinct sea creatures are plentiful. Manitoba is crisscrossed by rivers, many of them formed as the ice sheet melted. There are over 100,000 lakes, too, and the largest of these— Lakes Manitoba, Winnipeg, and Winnipegosis—are direct descendents of Lake Agassiz.

From the end of June to mid-September, over 3,000 beluga whales gather at the estuary where the Churchill River empties into Hudson Bay. They come to feed and give birth before retreating into Canada's high Arctic for the winter. Nicknamed "sea canaries," belugas chirp, whistle, click, squeak, and moo to communicate with each other and track their prey. They often swim close to boats, sometimes nudging them gently and twisting their heads as if stopping to say hello.

B also stands for bison. Known as the "supermarket of the plains" because it provided First Nations people with food, tools, and other necessities, the bison is honoured for its role in Manitoba's history and appears on both the provincial flag and its emblem.

Brandon, second largest city in Manitoba, is another **B**. Located in the southwest corner of the province in the heart of the grain-growing district, Brandon is called "Canada's Wheat City."

B is for Beluga whales
who click and squeal and sing
and sometimes turn their heads
to share a friendly greeting.

As the snow melts in spring, a small miracle happens in Manitoba. Clusters of delicate-looking purple flowers with yellow centers emerge from the cold ground, popping up in cheerful patches on the prairie and in dry, open wooded areas. It's the prairie crocus, a plant chosen in 1906 by the school children of Manitoba to be the province's floral emblem.

The crocus sometimes appears while there is still snow on the ground. To keep warm, it comes with its own fur coat and built-in solar panels. Tiny hairs cover the stem and leaves, and five petals reflect sunlight towards the flower's centre. Temperatures inside the flower can be as much as 10°C warmer than the outside air.

C is also for the Costume Museum of Canada. Located in Winnipeg, this one-of-a-kind museum has over 35,000 costumes and artifacts on display dating from the 1700s.

Each spring, our C, the Crocus
puts on a colourful show—
popping up in purple patches
in places still covered with snow.

Myrtle warbler, northern waterthrush, least flycatcher...these and more than 300 other bird species use Delta Marsh as a stopover during migration season. Located at the south end of Lake Manitoba, Delta Marsh is a wide band of protected wetland, one of the world's largest marshes, and the summer breeding grounds for waterfowl like Canada geese and mallard ducks. Delta Marsh is also a major refuelling spot for exotic songbirds on their way to other destinations. Well stocked with fish, insects, and grasses, Delta Marsh is paradise for birds. For bird-watching enthusiasts and scientists from around the world, it's a rare opportunity to study our feathered neighbours up close.

Manitoba has other protected wetland sites, too. Oak Hammock Marsh Interpretive Centre, 20 minutes north of Winnipeg, offers educational programs as well as trails that take visitors into the marsh. During migration season, Oak Hammock is a bustling place with numbers of waterfowl sometimes topping 400,000 daily.

Dd

Dis for Delta Marsh—
a kind of landing-strip
where our feathered friends stop a while
on their yearly migration trip.

I'm equal to any fella.
So said our **E**—Ella Cora Hind
who fought for fair and equal rights
so no one would be left behind.

In 1882 when Ella Cora Hind moved to Winnipeg from Ontario, women had few rights or opportunities. As a farm reporter with the *Manitoba Free Press*, Ella was respected for her predictions of crop and livestock production, forecasts that were so accurate they were used to set agricultural prices around the world. But Ella was more than a journalist. She was also a tireless fighter for reform.

Recognizing injustices in the political and social systems of her day, Ella targeted change. With Dr. Amelia Yeomans, she established the Manitoba Equal Franchise Club, and worked tirelessly to improve conditions in factories and prisons. Then, with Nellie McClung and Lillian Beynon Thomas, she founded the Political Equality League, an organization which campaigned for the right of women to vote. In 1916, Manitoba became the first province in Canada to grant women voting rights, thanks in part to Ella Cora Hind's vision of fair and just treatment for all.

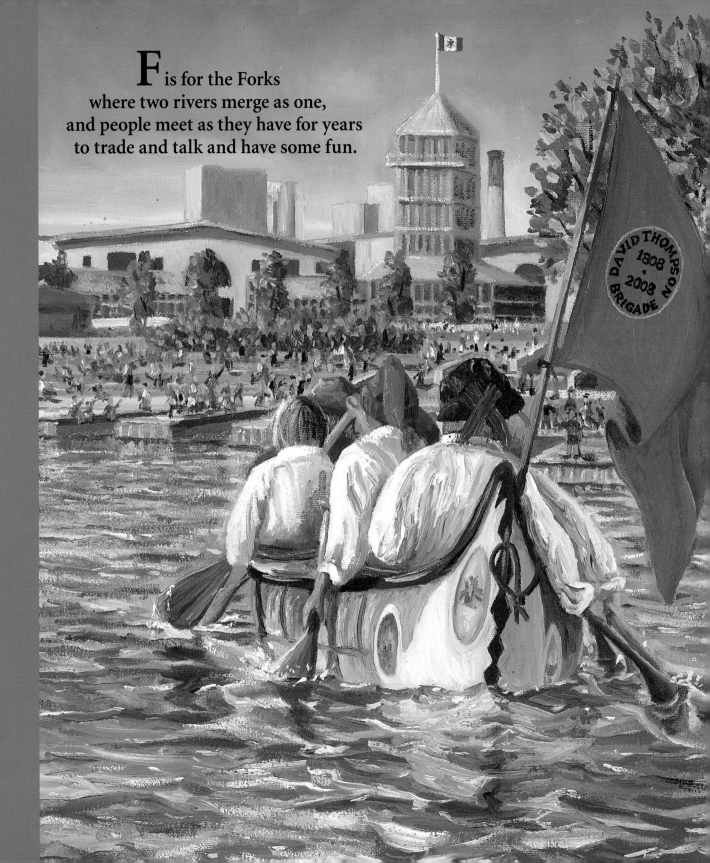

Winnipeg's two major rivers—the Red and the Assiniboine—meet near the city's centre at a spot known as the Forks.

For over 6,000 years, the Forks has been a meeting place for people. As early as 4,000 B.C., First Nations people migrating from northern forests to southern plains stopped at this place to rest, trade, and gather supplies. Later, European fur traders built forts there and used the rivers to carry furs and supplies between the Forks and trading posts hundreds of kilometres away. As Winnipeg grew, the Forks became a connecting hub for the railway system, earning it the nickname "Gateway to the Canadian West." In 1989 the Forks was declared a national historic site and was redeveloped into its present form—a busy complex of walkways, shops, restaurants, museums, and theatres.

Across the river from the Forks is another **F**, the French Quarter, a district with unique architecture and the largest concentration of French speaking Canadians outside of Quebec.

Ff

F is for the Forks
where two rivers merge as one,
and people meet as they have for years
to trade and talk and have some fun.

Our **G** is for the Golden Boy
who stands frozen in mid-run—
facing north, torch held high
glittering in the sun.

G g

Perched on the dome of the Manitoba Legislative Building in Winnipeg is the Golden Boy, a 5.25 metre statue. Made of bronze and gilded with 24 karat gold, the 1,650 kilogram statue looks like a youthful runner leading a race. In his right arm, the Golden Boy carries a torch and in his left, a sheaf of wheat. He faces north, the region where many natural resources are located.

The Golden Boy was cast in a Paris foundry at the height of World War I. It circled the Atlantic Ocean in the hold of a commandeered ship for months before finally arriving in Winnipeg. On November 21, 1919 the statue was hoisted to the top of the dome. Except for a brief period of restoration in 2002, it has stood proudly ever since.

G is also for great grey owl, Manitoba's provincial bird, and the largest owl in North America.

H stands for Heritage Festivals
    where Manitobans dance and sing
  to celebrate their different roots
and the many riches they bring.

Manitoba is a blend of many peoples with different customs and traditions. Numerous festivals celebrate the province's rich heritage. The largest is Winnipeg's Folklorama, a two week extravaganza every August featuring over 40 pavilions, each offering food, music, dance, and information from different countries.

There are scads of other festivals around the province, too, enough to keep those in a party mood busy. Visitors can toss cabers in Scottish fashion at Selkirk's Manitoba Highland Gathering, don Viking helmets at Gimli's Icelandic Festival, race dog-sleds at the Festival du Voyageur in St. Boniface, fiddle and jig at St. Laurent's Métis Days, taste Mennonite home cooking at Winkler's Harvest Festival, and clap along with dancing cossacks at Dauphin's National Ukrainian Festival. But these are just a few examples. The list of festivals around Manitoba is as long and as varied as its people.

Hh

I i

I stands for northern Ice Roads
which are an amazing thing—
appearing like magic in winter
disappearing again in spring.

Lakes, rivers, muskeg, and bog separate many of Manitoba's northern communities, making transportation by land a challenge. In summer, boats and planes are used to keep remote communities connected, but for up to eight weeks from mid-January to sometimes early March, a 2,200-kilometre network of temporary ice roads is used instead.

Construction of the ice roads starts after the first snowfall. Snowmobiles mark 60 metre-wide trails by packing down the snow on both land and ice so that frost can penetrate deeply. Trees are placed to mark the route across long lake stretches. Then, with each new snowfall, graders and snowploughs scrape away excess snow, keeping a thin layer to reflect sunlight so the road remains frozen. As the ice thickens, it becomes sturdy enough to support freight trucks carrying loads of up to 36,500 kilograms.

I also stands for the Inglis Grain Elevators National Historic Site where you can see five vintage prairie grain elevators, the last of their kind in Canada.

As a young boy, Jackson Beardy lived in Island Lake, a northern community. He had a close relationship with his grandmother who told him legends of his Cree ancestors. At the age of 7, he was sent to a government residential school near Winnipeg. Separated from his family and familiar surroundings, Jackson sought refuge in art and discovered through painting not only relief from isolation, but also a way of connecting with his roots. Using flowing black lines, sweeping bands of warm colours, and transparent-looking mythical figures, Jackson painted the stories he'd heard as a boy using a style that was all his own.

Jackson Beardy's paintings introduced others to native culture, and today they can be found in homes and galleries around the world. A tribute to Jackson Beardy, a giant mural based on a design he completed before his death in 1984, can be seen on the walls of the Indian Family Centre in Winnipeg.

Jj

J is for Jackson Beardy
who used color, lines that flow,
and images striking and bold
to paint stories told a long time ago.

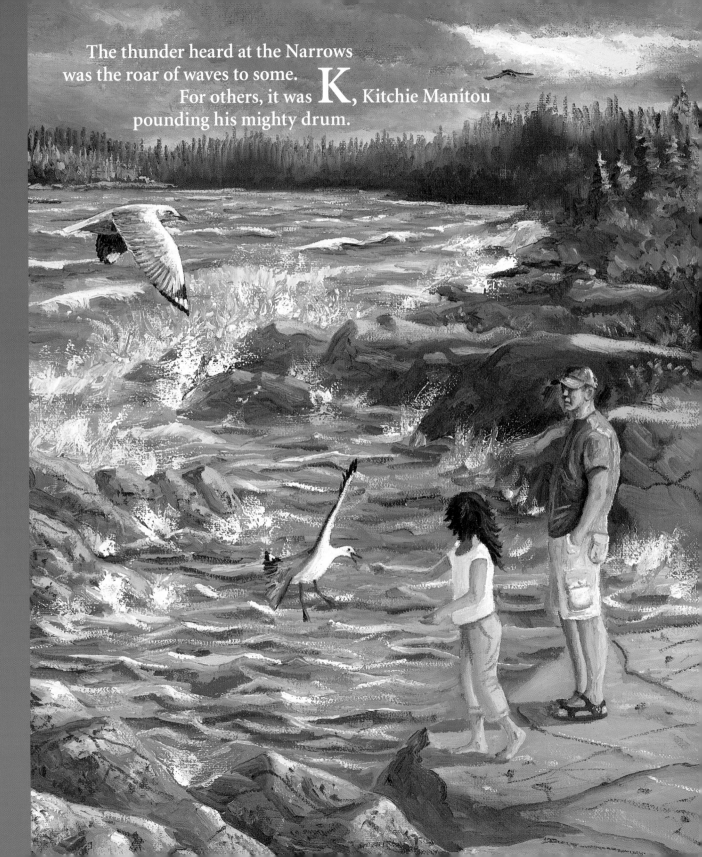

The thunder heard at the Narrows was the roar of waves to some. For others, it was **K**, Kitchie Manitou pounding his mighty drum.

Stand along the shore of Lake Manitoba at the Narrows, the place where the lake thins to less than a kilometre wide, and listen. On windswept days, you can hear waves crashing against loose limestone rocks along the north shore. To the aboriginal people who lived nearby, the sound had special significance. They believed it was Kitchie Manitou, the Great Spirit, pounding on a huge drum.

Although opinions differ, the name "Manitoba" likely has its origins in this early belief. In Cree, *manitou* means "Great Spirit" and *wapow* means "narrows." Joined together they become the "narrows of the Great Spirit"—*Manitou-bau*.

K also stands for kettle stones, large sandstone boulders which can be seen in only one place—Kettle Stones Provincial Park.

Another **K** is speed skater Cindy Klassen, winner of six Olympic medals, the most of any athlete in Canada.

Check a map of Manitoba.
See all the land, the lakes, too?
You'll find L, Lake Winnipeg, there
our largest patch of blue.

The largest of Manitoba's 100,000 lakes is Lake Winnipeg, a long, shallow body of water that stretches 425 kilometres south to north across the province. With an area of 24,500 square kilometres, it is the sixth largest lake in Canada and the most noticeable feature on maps of the province.

Lake Winnipeg is dotted with islands, many remote and undeveloped, and the shoreline is sprinkled with sandy beaches, limestone cliffs, and stands of boreal forest. With many rivers flowing into and out of it, Lake Winnipeg is a giant mixing machine for water from all over North America. An important source of fish and hydroelectric power, the south end is also a vacation playground, popular with sun-seekers and cottage dwellers. Grand Beach, world famous for its three kilometres of fine white sand, is a favourite destination. So, too, is the town of Gimli, home to the largest Icelandic population outside of Iceland.

Ll

M is for the mighty Mosasaur—
fierce hunter and awesome brute
with pinpoint teeth, lightning speed
and hearty appetite to boot.

One of the most vicious creatures living in the sea that once covered much of Manitoba was a lizard-like reptile known as the mosasaur. Streamlined for swimming with paddle-shaped fins and a powerful tail, the mosasaur was capable of extreme bursts of speed. A ferocious hunter, the mosasaur could outswim most prey, and, with its double-hinged jaw, flexible skull, and rows of conical teeth, gulp down many whole.

Fossils of mosasaurs as well as other extinct sea creatures have been unearthed around Morden, Manitoba. Many are on display at the Canadian Fossil Discovery Centre there, including "Bruce," a 13-metre mosasaur, the largest found in Canada.

M also stands for Manipogo, a legendary serpent said to live in Lake Manitoba. Although sightings of the creature have been reported, no definite proof of its existence has ever been found.

At **N**, the Narcisse Snake Dens—
just watch where you walk or run.
In spring the earth wriggles with reptiles
all seeking their share of the sun.

At the end of April or in early May, after the snow disappears, the ground around Narcisse, Manitoba, wriggles to life. Attracted by the sun's warmth, more than 50,000 red-sided garter snakes—the largest concentration of snakes in the world—crawl outside from winter dens deep inside the earth. The non-poisonous snakes gather around den openings, males usually emerging first. When a female appears, dozens of males converge, wrapping themselves around her to make a tight, writhing bundle known as a "mating ball." The mating phenomenon continues for up to three weeks, then the snakes disperse, fanning out to gardens, fields, and wetlands in the area. In the late fall, the snakes migrate back to the dens where they spend the winter in frost-free areas far below the ground.

The spring mating ritual draws over 20,000 curious visitors from around the world, all eager to witness one of nature's most unusual events.

In the northern city of Thompson, a 10-storey painting of a wolf gazes from the side of an apartment block. In Boissevain, 20 colourful murals on the town's buildings depict the community's history and culture. Across Manitoba, large-scale art like this is alive and well and visible outdoors.

But it's not only colossal paintings that adorn our province. The town of Selkirk has Chuck the Channel Cat, a 7.6-metre tall sculpture of a grinning catfish; Steinbach has a 12-metre long Rolls Royce; and Lundar has a massive Canada goose. There are over 40 super-sized statues on display around Manitoba. Some are record holders. The largest Coca-Cola™ can in existence can be found in Portage la Prairie; the world's largest painting on an easel stands in Altona; the largest crocus sculpture is in Arden; the biggest pumpkin sculpture ever is in Roland.

Each outdoor giant tells a little about the town's people and its attractions, and in friendly Manitoba fashion, invites visitors to stay a while.

In Manitoba, giants greet you
    on walls, along roads, around the bend—
O in sculptures enormous, paintings glorious
   stands for Outdoor Art, my friend.

P is for Polar bears
who linger around Hudson Bay,
attracting hordes of visitors
while they wait for cooler days.

P p

Churchill, Manitoba is famous for its autumn visitors. Each October and November, polar bears take up temporary residence on the outskirts of this small northern town as they wait for the ice to freeze on Hudson Bay. The polar bears attract other visitors, too. Tourists flock to the town, anxious to catch a glimpse of the lumbering white beasts, giving Churchill its other name—"Polar Bear Capital of the World."

Once winter arrives, the bears head across the ice and linger around breathing holes, waiting for seals—their primary food source—to surface. In spring, as the ice melts, the bears move back to shore to stalk other prey on land.

Polar bears are endangered creatures. With climate change, the ice is now thinner and lasts for shorter periods. Longer stretches of open water separate ice floes, making it more difficult for polar bears to survive.

All aboard! **P** also stands for Prairie Dog Central Railway, one of the oldest operating steam trains in North America.

Manitoba has rich deposits of rocks and minerals, and the province is peppered with quarries, pits, and mines where the material is dug, blasted, or chiselled out of the ground. Limestone is especially plentiful, thanks to the inland sea that covered much of the province. As creatures in the sea died, the calcium carbonate in their skeletons became part of the muddy bottom, eventually hardening into rock. A unique type of mottled-looking limestone known as Tyndall Stone is quarried near Garson, Manitoba. Embedded inside the stone are fossils of corals, brachiopods, trilobites and other sea creatures. Tyndall Stone has been used in buildings across North America, including Manitoba's own legislative building and the parliament buildings in Ottawa.

Visitors can learn more about the quarrying process at Quarry Park in Stonewall, an abandoned quarry complete with massive kilns and interpretive trails.

Search the rocks, scan the stones
at Q for Quarry, you never know.
Deep inside there might be treasure—
a fossil from long ago.

R is for Louis Riel,
Métis leader, determined and strong
who led his people in rebellion
to right what he thought was wrong.

Born in 1844, Louis Riel was a Métis—a person of mixed aboriginal and European ancestry. Well-educated and a skilled speaker, Riel fought to protect the rights, language, and culture of the Métis at the time when Manitoba was poised to become a province.

As a champion of the Métis, Riel led two rebellions. The first eventually led to the creation of a new province, Manitoba, but a second in Saskatchewan ended with Riel's surrender. He was convicted of treason, and despite much opposition, was executed as a traitor on November 16, 1885.

In 1992, the Parliament of Canada revoked Riel's conviction. Now, rather than being viewed as a traitor, Louis Riel is considered to be the "Father of Manitoba" for the role he played in helping to establish Manitoba as a province.

R is also for Riding Mountain National Park, an oasis of lakes, hills, and trees located in south-central Manitoba.

At **S** for Spirit Sands,
the dunes spread high and wide.
For you, it's a great place to visit
for the skink, a great place to hide.

Between the towns of Glenboro and Carberry, alongside the Assiniboine River, a patch of sand climbs out of the flat prairie. It's an unexpected sight, appearing out of nowhere, a rolling carpet of golden sand where you'd expect to find grass and trees instead. If you're lucky, you might see a northern prairie skink, for this is where Manitoba's only lizard lives.

Welcome to Spirit Sands, an awe-inspiring wonder of nature. The dunes—some 30 metres high—are evidence of time's shifting ways. Thousands of years ago, when Lake Agassiz drained, it left this sea of sand behind. Once covering an area of 6,500 square kilometres, today only 4 square kilometres remain. Trees have made steady inroads, reclaiming the land as their own.

West of Spirit Sands, you'll find another **S**. The Souris Swinging Bridge is the longest suspension bridge in Canada.

Ss

In Manitoba, there are many **T**s—
*T*rees, *t*rails, and *t*rout are samples.
But if it's history and mystery you want
Turtle Mountain is the perfect example.

T *t*

The Turtle Mountain area straddles the Manitoba-North Dakota border, running 70 kilometres east-to-west, and rising 240 metres above the surrounding prairie. Formed at the end of the last Ice Age by retreating glaciers, Turtle Mountain is the oldest occupied region of the province, inhabited for almost 10,000 years by First Nations like the Sioux, Dakota, and Algonquin. Turtle Mountain is steeped in ancient legend, and peppered with burial mounds, stone circles, and arrowheads. Rich in forests and lakes, the Turtle Mountain region is home to moose, white-tailed deer, beaver, raccoon, and yes, even turtles.

At the western side of Turtle Mountain, along the border between Canada and the United States, lies the International Peace Garden. A 9.46 square kilometre preserve of floral displays, sunken gardens, fountains, and towering structures, the Peace Garden is a symbol of the friendship that unites the two countries.

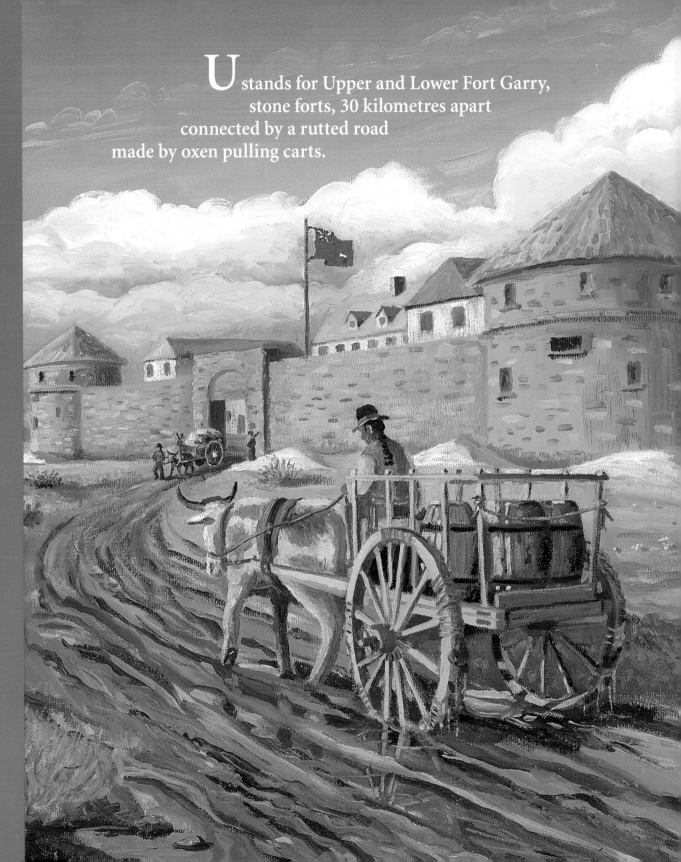

Uu

U stands for Upper and Lower Fort Garry, stone forts, 30 kilometres apart connected by a rutted road made by oxen pulling carts.

In 1821 the Hudson Bay Company built Fort Garry in the heart of present-day Winnipeg. In 1826 flooding destroyed the fort, and a replacement constructed out of Tyndall Stone was built on higher ground, 30 kilometres north along the Red River near Selkirk. To reach the new Fort Garry required a long journey for settlers in the south, however, and in 1835, another, more convenient Fort Garry was built at the Forks. Situated upstream, the new fort was called Upper Fort Garry, and the downstream fort near Selkirk, Lower Fort Garry.

Traffic between the two forts was brisk. Red River carts towed by oxen travelling side-by-side—sometimes 20 across—carved a rutted road 36 metres wide in places. Today that road is one of Winnipeg's busiest and widest—Main Street.

Of Upper Fort Garry, only the North Gate remains. However, Lower Fort Garry stands intact. Perched high above the Red River, it is a national historic site and the oldest stone fur-trading post in North America.

Frederick William Hall lived on Pine Street in Winnipeg. So did Leo Clarke. Robert Shankland, too. The three men lived in the 700 block of the tree-lined street, but their connection goes further. It lies in the trenches of Belgium and France, in the blood and muck of war, and in the individual acts of heroism for which the three men are known.

During World War I, the three enlisted in the Canadian Army and served overseas. The men distinguished themselves with separate acts of bravery. Although out-numbered and severely injured, Clarke single-handedly held off an enemy attack. Hall died rescuing a wounded man in the heat of battle. Acting alone, Shankland crawled through enemy lines to deliver critical information to the Allies.

For their acts of courage, the three men were awarded the Victoria Cross, the highest honour possible, and to further remember their deeds Pine Street was renamed Valour Road, the name it bears today.

Vv

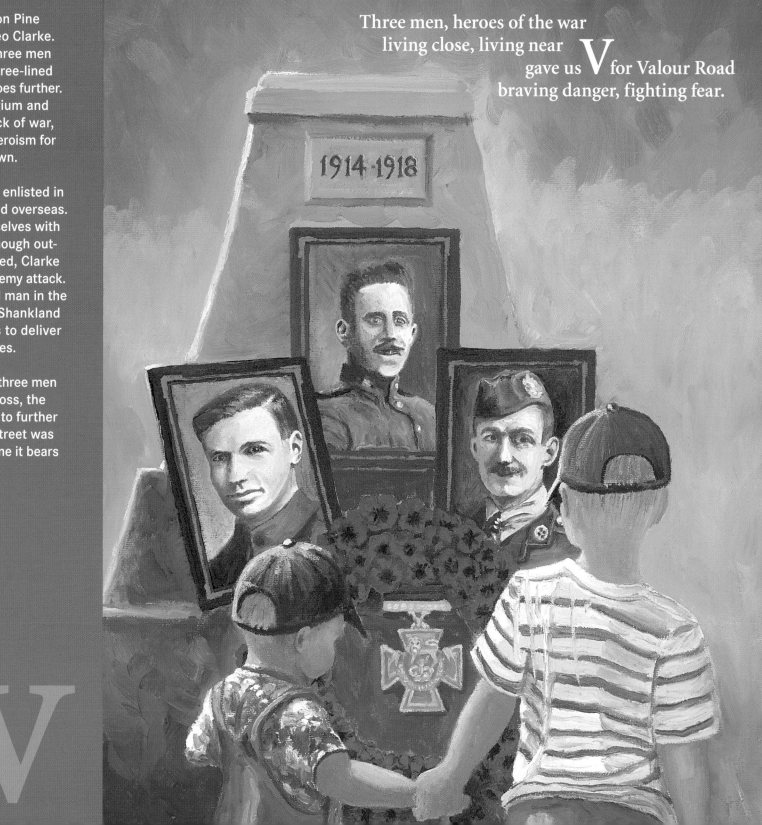

Three men, heroes of the war
living close, living near
gave us V for Valour Road
braving danger, fighting fear.

Whiteshell Provincial Park, in the southeastern corner of the province, is Manitoba's largest provincial park. Featuring clear lakes, rushing rivers, thick stands of spruce forest, and rocky outcroppings of Precambrian Shield, the Whiteshell is a popular destination for leisure activities. One of its most unique formations is West Hawk Lake, an unusually deep lake formed eons ago when a meteorite ploughed into the bedrock. The eastern section of the Whiteshell is home to a large wolf population as well as the 63 kilometre Mantario Trail, the province's longest hiking trail.

W also stands for white spruce, Manitoba's provincial tree. With an average life-span of 200 years, this hardy tree can be found in most regions of the province.

Another **W** is wild rice, a grassy plant which grows in shallow slow-moving waters in northern and eastern areas. Manitoba is one of the largest suppliers of this nutritious grain.

Wis for Whiteshell Provincial Park.
Wilderness beauty, rising high, dipping low
filled with rocks and trees and twisting trails
around the lakes formed so long ago.

Walking through the Exchange District of Winnipeg is like stepping into the past. In this section of the city's downtown, almost 150 vintage buildings, many at least a century old, stand side-by-side in tidy rows. Most of the buildings are constructed of brick, marble, or Tyndall Stone, and were once banks, warehouses, or industrial shops. Some are decorated with gothic carvings. Others have iron wrought balconies, stone columns, and graceful mouldings.

During the late 1800s and early 1900s when many of these structures were built, Winnipeg was a bustling hub of manufacturing and financial exchange. As the city grew and evolved, the buildings served other purposes, but their looks remained largely the same.

In 1997, the Exchange District, with its one-of-a-kind architecture, was declared a national historic site. Today, it is the centre of culture and entertainment in the city, home to theatres, galleries, shops, nightclubs, and restaurants. The area is popular with film-makers, too, and often serves as a backdrop for movies needing a turn-of-the-century look.

Twenty blocks at the city's heart
X with buildings a century old,
is for the Exchange District
where goods were traded and sold.

Xx

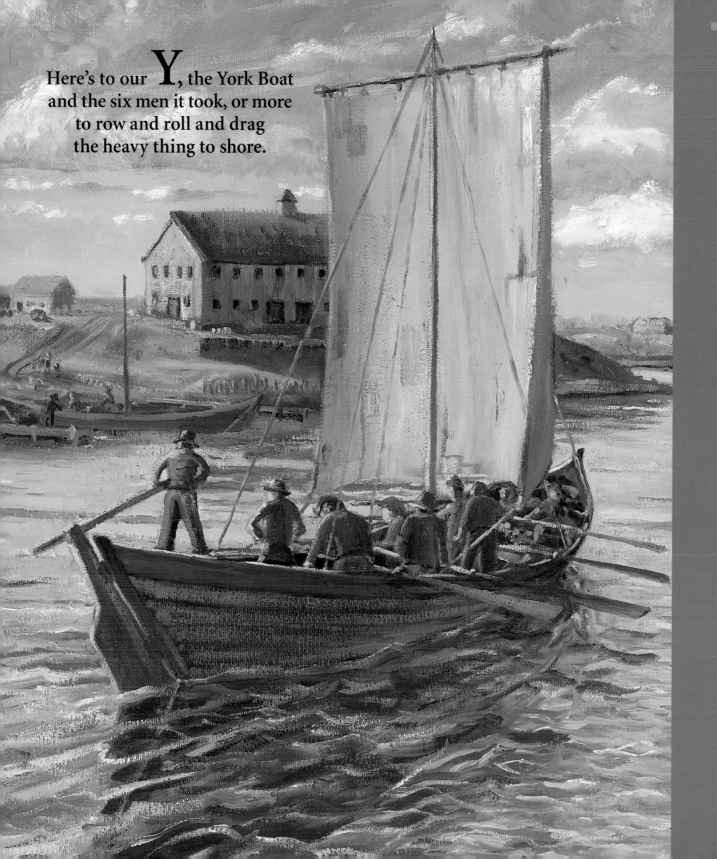

Here's to our **Y**, the York Boat
and the six men it took, or more
to row and roll and drag
the heavy thing to shore.

Yy

Between 1749 and the 1880s, a wooden vessel known as the York Boat ruled the waterways of Manitoba. Named after York Factory, the Hudson Bay Company headquarters where it was first made, the York Boat was used to transport supplies between the company's outposts. With its flat, broad bottom, planked sides, and pointed bow, the 12-metre-long York Boat resembled a Viking ship shrunken down in size. Equipped with both oars and a square sail, and operated by a crew of six to eight men, the York Boat was steady in rough waters and more reliable than a canoe. Its main disadvantage was its weight and size. Too heavy to carry across portages, the York boat and its load had to be dragged overland using a system of ropes and rollers.

The York Boat is remembered at the northern community of Norway House where aluminium replicas race against each other in a celebration known as Treaty & York Boat Days.

During the Flood of the Century
Manitobans stood their ground
by building our Z, the Z-dike
to zigzag the water around.

Along the Red River Valley spring flooding is a frequent threat. Fed by melting snow, the Red and its tributaries swell and sometimes overflow their banks. To protect Winnipeg, a massive ditch was constructed to divert water around the city during floods. Since its completion in 1968, the Red River Floodway has saved the city many times, but in 1997, a year of especially rapid and severe snow melt, the Floodway was put to the ultimate test. With water rising quickly and the Floodway filling to capacity, a new dike was hastily built, slapped together out of clay, crushed rock and 3,000 kilogram sandbags, then topped by dozens of derelict buses and cars hauled from wrecking yards. The 42 kilometre dike zigzagged across fields and roads, earning it the nickname "Z-Dike." After the waters receded, the temporary dike was dismantled, but the "Z-Dike" lingers in the memories of Manitobans, reminding them of their resourcefulness during a very difficult time.

Z z

A Red River Cart Full of Questions

1. What lake covered much of Manitoba 20,000 years ago?

2. Where is the oldest inhabited area of Manitoba?

3. Where is the National Ukrainian Festival held every year?

4. Five of them stand at Inglis, Manitoba. What are they?

5. Where did the Golden Boy spend most of 1918-1919?

6. Name the two rivers that meet at The Forks in Winnipeg.

7. What are the polar bears of Churchill waiting for each October and November?

8. What makes Tyndall Stone so unique?

9. Who is called the 'Father of Manitoba'?

10. Why are beluga whales called 'sea canaries'?

11. Who is 'Bruce', and where was he found?

12. Where does Manitoba's only lizard, the northern prairie skink, live?

13. What is unique about West Hawk Lake in Whiteshell Provincial Park?

14. What was added to the top of the Z-Dike during the 'Flood of the Century'?

15. How many female Red-sided Garter Snakes are in a 'mating ball'?

16. Usually how long do ice roads last?

17. Where are 'The Narrows'?

18. Name Manitoba's three largest lakes.

19. To see the world's largest Coke can, where would you go?

20. How was the York Boat portaged over land?

21. Where is 'Canada's Wheat City'?

22. What beach along Lake Winnipeg is famous for its fine white sand?

Answers

1. Lake Agassiz

2. Around the Turtle Mountain region in the southwest part of the province

3. Dauphin, Manitoba

4. Vintage grain elevators, the last surviving row in Canada.

5. In the hold of a ship criss-crossing the Atlantic Ocean.

6. The Red and Assiniboine.

7. For the ice to freeze on Hudson Bay.

8. It is mottled-looking and embedded with fossils of extinct sea creatures.

9. Louis Riel

10. Because of the distinctive chirping, squealing, and popping sounds they make.

11. Bruce is Canada's largest fossil mosasaur. He was found near Morden, Manitoba and is on display at the Canadian Fossil Discovery Centre there.

12. At Spirit Sands

13. It is unusually deep, and was formed by a meteorite long ago.

14. Derelict vehicles hauled from wrecking yards

15. Just one. The rest are males.

16. Although the life-span of ice roads varies with climate conditions, normally they last about eight weeks, from mid-January to early March.

17. At the narrowest part of Lake Manitoba

18. Lakes Winnipeg, Manitoba & Winnipegosis.

19. Portage la Prairie

20. Too heavy to carry, the York Boat had to be rolled, towed, dragged and pushed over the ground.

21. Brandon, Manitoba

22. Grand Beach

Larry Verstraete

Larry Verstraete, a native Manitoban, grew up in the French Quarter of Winnipeg, a stone's throw from the Golden Boy. A former teacher, he now spends his time writing, visiting young readers in schools and libraries, and presenting at conferences and festivals. *G is for Golden Boy* is his eighth book for young people, and his first picture book.

Brian Lund

After graduating with a degree in Environmental Design from the University of Manitoba, Brian Lund spent the early years of his career surveying in rural Manitoba, indulging his love for nature and the outdoors. Traveling, camping, hiking, and cycling have always been favourite pastimes. Since retiring in 2003 from a career in digital mapping at the City of Winnipeg, he works most days in his Winnipeg studio or outdoors gathering inspiration for new artistic works. Brian is a self taught artist. He welcomed the opportunity to illustrate his first book, *G is for Golden Boy: A Manitoba Alphabet.*